BUILDING SUCCESS IN LIFE

Achieving inner mind

James Ngozi Okere

+2347035289205 & +2348052169045
E-mail: jmsokere@gmail.com

www.inspireforgreatness.com

ISBN: --------------------------------

FIRST PUBLISHED IN 2018

DEDICATION

Dedicated to all those who have built success story and risen to greatness through belief in ideas and in themselves. It is also dedicated to all those who read this book and painstakingly pursue a cause to achieve success in life, attested to by humanity and society.

ACKNOWLEDGMENT

The supports I got from my previous works were instrumental to the publication of this book: Building Success in life.

I received tremendous supports from Mrs. Adelyn Nkechi Okere (my lovely wife); to her and indeed my family, I remain ever grateful. To Odinakachukwu Onwuatuogu-my online assistant, I thank you immensely.

I acknowledge the inputs made by inspirational authors, speakers and writers, whose works I have come across. These people include Brian Tracy, Dr. Myles Munroe, Pastor Oral Roberts, Napoleon Hill, Pastor John C. Maxwell, Pastor Mike Murdock and Joyce Meyer. Others are Dr. Ben Carson, Pastor Benny Hinn , Bill Newman, John Mason, Rev. Dr. Chris E. Kwakpovwe, Norman Vincent Peale, Robert H. Schuller, Pastor T.D Jakes, Pastor David Ibiyeomie, Pastor Joel Osteen, Udo Okonjo, Daniel Ally, Ajah Mishara etc. I owe them greatly for spurring me to write this book.

Finally, I am grateful to my lovely wife, Mrs. Adelyn N. Okere, Public Servant, Administrator and a great companion and supporter towards my vision; she contributed immensely to the making of this book, including writing the foreword.

James Ngozi Okere

FOREWORD

It is a great joy being invited by one's husband to write foreword of her husband's book; "Building Success In Life". I am aware that my husband invited me because I have been part of his blogging journey and the publication of his previous three books; You Too Can Be Great, Developing Yourself and How To Excel Life, these books he authored by the grace of God; a journey that has not been easy for him.

At present the author is a Public Speaker, an Inspirational Blogger, Social Entrepreneur, Lead Consultant of Inspire Foundation (IF) Leadership and Mentorship Academy, and Project Coordinator of Inspire Foundation (IF), a Non-Governmental Organization; aimed at inculcating positive values in the youth for self realization and advancement for a better society .

Building Success In Life is another motivational and inspirational book written out of the author's experiences in his core area of life. The book is a success challenging one, motivator and influencer geared towards driving one to realize his calling in life.

In Chapter One, the author identified and presented two key issues; vision and courage as the twin power of success in one's life. In Chapter Two, he went further to identify the required winning attitude that a person should demonstrate in the pursuits of success.

In Chapter Three, the inspirational blogger highlighted the God factor in building success in life; which he stated is of paramount.

In Chapter Four, under the mind of achievers, the author revealed the values that propel a person into prominence in life. While in Chapter Five, he raised the issues bordering on Building Success In a Personality.

In Chapter Six titled Building Success Through The Power Of Action, the author shared the thoughts and experiences of people on the need to embrace taken action as key towards building success in life.

In Chapter Seven, he opined that dream pursuits is important if successes are to be recorded by one on this planet earth.

Also, in Chapter Eight, Chapter Nine and Chapter Ten, the author admonished all to Develop his/her Personality, Become An Influencer and Work to Become An Impact Person respectively.

The author in Chapter Eleven identified that Pressing On To Your Mark; is a sure way to succeed, while in chapter Twelve, he emphasized on the need to embrace the Power Of Commitment In Building Success

In Chapter Thirteen, he wrote on Become the Success Story; a challenge indeed, while in Chapter Fourteen, the public speaker captured the story of his Blogging Journey: to end this inspiring book- Building Success In Life. I recommend this book to all who would want to improve their image in life and by so doing impact the society.

Mrs. Adelyn N. Okere,
Public Servant and Administrator.

INTRODUCTION:

There is no body on this planet earth who does not desire to become successful. Everybody would want to be described as a great person in a chosen career or profession. From beginning God created man to become a success story. God instructed us in the Holy Bile to become fruitful on this planet earth. Fruitfulness means to live a life of accomplishments attested to by the society. Thus a successful person attains a special height in the society. The person is acknowledged, recognized, and admired. The person becomes a role model in the society. By God's instruction on achieving success, it means that there is the God factor in the life of anyone who would want to achieve greatness.

Building success in life is a journey. It is a journey of trials and failures. It is a journey of ups and downs. It is a journey of denials. It is a journey of developing one's personality. It is a journey of building one's talents, gifts and abilities in life. In this journey, if one did not give up, success is assured as God rewards hard work.

"The first step towards success is taken when you refuse to be a captive of the environment in which you first find yourself" (Mahatma Gandhi).

Therefore, building success in life has both the spiritual and physical connotations. The spiritual gives confirmation that God from the beginning approved man to become an achiever. The Holy Bible recorded that a man who works diligently shall stand before great people. It further stated that God gives power to make wealth.

On the other hand, the human angle of building success in life opined that one must make conscious efforts if one must succeed in life. This is where the success values of life come in. These values are vision, hard work, persistence, determination, prayer etc. Therefore, in all totality, achieving success must embrace both the spiritual and human angle factors. Both must strike a balance and work complimentarily.

Successes can be achieved through developing a dream, working on the vision developed. In addition, to succeed we must develop a heart of prayer to enable us have equipped conquering spirits. Seeking information by one is also a sure way to achieve greatness. Success comes also through locating a mentor; this is what also raised James Owen to greater height in sports. Many years ago, James Owen wanted to become a great athlete in Europe. He sorts for the view of his coach; who gave him four keys to stardom: determination, dedication, discipline and attitude. James Owen started working on them. At the 1923 Berlin Olympics he got four gold medals and his record in long jump lasted for 25 years unbroken. He did not just have a goal, but he applied himself to the four vital keys for success.

The same success values listed above, and in addition to having commitment and endurance spirits were values that gave Tyler Perry (famed playwright, director, actor and producer) success, fame, honour, elevation in his profession. To make it to Hollywood filmmaking was difficult. It would have led him to give up but he continued, and being a black worsened his case towards realizing his destiny in the area of film producing. Tyler Perry was from New Orleans's Seventh Ward. He fought a battle, built his success carrier path, developed a heart of an achiever and he succeeded.

At the age of twenty-two, Tyler wrote, directed and produced many stage plays that were financed with his personal savings. For more performances than he could count, only a handful of people showed up. This went on for years, but he persevered. He continued to save and invest his own money to produce the plays, but nothing seemed to take off and he remained patient with his destiny. Even when the cast performed to nearly empty house, Tyler never let go of his dream. He powered his dream and battled all obstacles to produce another play, even when no one had come to the previous one.

Tyler was even ridiculed by the Hollywood executives who told him, they could not back his movie because "Black people don't go to the movies". He held on and refused to let go of his dream to write, direct, produce plays and movies.

Tyler was only fighting to keep his destiny; he wasn't fighting side battles of rejection, ridiculing etc. He invested his Warrior Spirit in fights that were worth the effort to get his plays and films produced. At a time he was homeless and slept in his automobile all in a bid to keep his dream alive. Because he never gave up, the winds of fate changed in his favour and he has since sold millions of theater and movies tickets to fans of his beloved Madea persona.

Tyler Perry made his brain work in the words of Kenyon E.W (author) who said **"Make your brain work, it will sweat, but make it work, then it will improve, it will develop, until you become the envy of those around you".** He remained tenacious towards his vision and he succeeded in his chosen profession.

Building success is indeed a journey. In as much we live in a hostile and discouraging environment, suffice it to say that greatness emanates highly from an

unfriendly environment; as great and tremendous accomplishments have been recorded during period of crises, trials and discouragements in one's life.

CHAPTER ONE.

THE TWIN POWER OF SUCCESS

Vision and Courage are twin inseparable values of greatness; they are twin power of building success in life. The two success values operate closely in life pursuit. Vision and Courage are two coins of the same face. Great achievements recorded are product of Vision and Courage. Extra-ordinary successes are as a result of extra-ordinary vision and courage demonstrated by men and women who are desirous to succeed in life.

Visions are (dreams and ideas) before it manifest physically. Courage therefore works with vision to make any dream or idea come into reality; thus leading towards recording achievements. Therefore, in building success in life, one should be ready to have a vision of life and the accompanying courage to make such vision or goal work.

In industries, the distinguishing factor from one industry or another or from one firm to another is vision and courage. Every promising and prospering industry or firm have clear vision of where they are going, and the accompanying courage to achieve such vision or dream. Vision is so important that any organization advertises her organizational goals anchored on her vision.

Also in governance, a distinguishing known factor in leadership is the power of vision and courage exhibited by the leadership. We often hear; this leadership has no vision or the leadership lacks courage to provide the needed leadership.

A leader can also have vision, but lacks the courage to implement the identified vision. An individual can also have vision (this exist always) but lacks the courage to execute such vision that would re-launch him in the society, or give him a turning point in life. This is where the journey of building success in life begins.

Courageous people start where other people have stopped in any particular venture. No, is not in their dictionary. They have the 'I can spirit'. They see where they are going rather than the obstacles on the way.

The power of vision when combined with courage is a driving force towards any success attested to by the society.

Reuben Martinez from Miami Arizona United States of America is one man who demonstrated great vision and courage towards promoting reading and literacy values in the world, thus he built success story in life.

Reuben's parents who were Mexican immigrants who worked in mines had no business in reading books. However, Reuben had vision towards reading. He admitted that his mother always wanted him to put down his book and clean the yard.

Following his interest in reading and literacy development, he went further to develop the required courage to continue, that even by 6.45 am every day, he would woke up and read his neighbor's newspapers brought by newspaper boy, thereafter, he folds back and kept the newspapers for the owner (his neighbour). His neighbour having seen Reuben's courage, went ahead to encourage Reuben.

Reuben's drive to succeed in life, through his vision and courage moved his teachers to assist him via lending him books. Reuben, later as opportunity came opened a barbershop, and continued with his visionary drive in literacy development leading to using his barbershop to start lending the books he had collected to people to read; Reuben later stopped lending books as borrowers stopped returning the borrowed books, rather now selling books which he started with only two books, he sold in 1983.

Powered by his success drive, he continued and became an advocate for literacy via his life vision and courage demonstrated by him. Few years later, the barbershop with books became a book store; which he called Libreria Martinez Books and Art Gallery which has grown tremendously.

By his industry, as at year 2007, the store now store up to seventeen thousand titles and has become one of the country's largest collections of Spanish Language books. He has also opened more books stores.

For his vision and courage to promote literacy, he stated hosting a weekly cable show on Univision. He cofounded the Latino Book Festival with actor Edward James Olmos. Reuben stated speaking at Schools and to other groups to promote literacy. As his vision and courage in this area increases, in 2004, he won a MacArthur Foundation fellowship often called a **"genius grant"**- for fusing the roles of market place and community centre to inspire appreciation of literacy and literature and preserve Latino Literacy heritage.

In addition, for his vision and courage, he received honourary doctorate in human letter from Whittier College in 2005, and was also named one of Inc.com's twenty-six most fascinating entrepreneurs.

Reuben Martinez vision and courage in life became tremendous leading to his achieving remarkable successes in global literacy development to prove that success is a journey and that one's dream is achievable through vision and demonstrable courage.

CHAPTER TWO.

DEVELOP A WINNING ATTITUDE

Building success in life requires a strong winning spirit. The saying that winners don't quit is indeed a reality. No success has ever been recorded in any spheres of life by quitters. In addition, no greatness has ever been accomplished by people who abandoned their idea. Historically, all winners are non-quitters in life. It is true that initially they can fail, but in their failing they further reshaped their thoughts for better accomplishments in future.

Therefore, winning attitude is a virtue that has to be developed by world changers and persons who are eager to build successful platform in life. These world changers are makers of history and they also create positive news for societal development.

The first principle that works with developing winning attitude is developing vision of life. Vision of life is planned goal(s) to be achieved. They are dream that one wants to champion as to direct the course of history in a positive way. This vision of life is the anchor base of all achievements in life. Dream or vision development must be activated with right values of life by success builders.

In addition, in developing a winning attitude towards building success in life, one must believe in him or herself. Believing in oneself gives strength and passion to pursue a task. If one believes in himself, he developed the right self esteem to power his dream or vision of life. Self esteem galvanizes self motivation and the strength in us; activating one towards obtaining success in life.

Winning attitude goes with great sense of determination. In this regard, one must have the courage to pursue a task of life. One who must build success must align with the Four Cs of courage. These four Cs of courage are courage to begin, courage to continue, courage to finish and courage to sustain. In any project towards building success in life, we must begin (if we do not begin, it can't work), we must continue (if we do not continue, the project stops), we must finish the task (if we stop on the way; the task is over) and finally if we do not sustain the task (all the efforts made are now wasted). If there is no sustainability growth, future developments stops; hence possible accomplishments are stopped on the way.

All known persons who built success story in life persevered. Persistence Napoleon Hill; the great author says ***"Truly if one has persistence one can get along very well without other qualities".*** The person who perseveres in a task must win. To conquer ups and downs of life endavours, one must develop persevering spirit; the drive to achieve. Men and women have had their dream aborted because they lacked the persevering virtue of life, thus perseverance is an attitude that must be developed by a heart desirous to succeed.

In addition, time is a resource; hence management of time must effectively be put into proper action. We all have 24 hours a day; and this 24 hours is a scarce commodity. Speaking on time Pastor Thomas Dexter Jakes writes "Time is our most valuable resource because it cannot be reproduced or replicated. Once it's gone, it's gone". A second lost, a minute lost; talk less hours lost cannot be regained back. It is said that you can recover millions of dollars lost, but you cannot recover several hours lost. Therefore a person desirous to build success in life must plan for effective utilization of the available time with great discipline.

In addition, to all of the above, hard work must be embraced as a factor towards developing a winning attitude. Hard work is the action or activity we put in towards realizing our vision or dream of life. To build success in life, we must work hard. Hard work breaks barriers and successes recorded with time. However, if we have sense of purpose, then hard work is better appreciated.

CHAPTER THREE.

THE GOD FACTOR IN BUILDING SUCCESS

The earth is a creation of God. Your personality is a creation of God. Thus the first principle towards building success in life will be walking in line with God's power. ***"The knowledge of God you have can determine the height that you can go in life. Praying and spending time with God will always assist one… If you learn to start your day early with God, you will find out that you will have a walk over, over other challenges"*** Prof. Olusola Onyewole, a former Vice Chancellor of the University of Agriculture Abeokuta, Ogun State Western Nigeria and a onetime Regional Overseer of the Mountain of Fire and Miracles Ministry for West Africa .

Also, Abraham Lincoln a former United States of America (U.S.A) President who contested election up to seven times before he recorded success recognized the spiritual dimension of building success in life when he said ***"Without the assistance of a Divine being, I cannot succeed. With that assistance, I cannot fail".***

Your success story as a persona is a creation of God. Thus the first principle towards developing one's personality is walking in line with God's power.

Some Biblical principles associated with building success in the life of a person include; God gives power to make wealth, with God all things are possible, commit thy ways unto God's hand, for He will bless them, whatever you sow, that you will reap, a man who works diligently shall stand before great people etc.

Thus many people have attested their greatness or success to God. It is clear that without God, dreams are aborted. Without God, ideas would die at conception. Without God, strength would not be available for any person to pursue meaningful project towards building a success story in life.

The success story of Zig Ziglar; a motivational author and speaker who was born into a rural agrarian family will further illustrate the God factor in building success in life. Ziglar's father died, when he was just five years, living him and his siblings with the mother. To survive, the family was involved in periodical part-time jobs. Even at the age of four, he was helping the family, and was also involved in milking cows before he was eight years.

He struggled with life until he had encounter with God who changed his world view and life. If not for God, Zig Ziglar would have been a frustrated person, and history would have no place for him. Today he is well recognized in USA and the world. To his credit he has authored many motivational books.

Ziglar's desire and dream to become a speaker was born in 1952, when he heard Bob Bale, a motivational speaker from Phoenix, Arizona U.S.A spoke at a seminar in Florence, South Carolina, U.S.A. Again to achieve his dream of being a motivational speaker was not easy at all. For sixteen years he struggled to get speaking engagements; however the support of the family and his wife encouraged him to continue in his quest. Ziglar admitted that the love of the wife and her prayers made the difference in his life, as he kept on believing God and also keeping a positive mental attitude to succeed.

On 4th July 1972 through, an interaction of an elderly African American woman who stayed in Ziglar's home, this woman talked about Jesus all the time, and Ziglar this time committed his life to Christ (though born into a Christian home and attended Church) and he became a new personality in Jesus. At the age of 45, Ziglar had a new beginning. His past attempts towards building succeed proved abortive, but all that changed when Christ came into his life, and he also became a tithing person.

His achievements grew that since 1972 he had not solicited a single engagement rather he had turned down engagements because his calendar was full. His business blossomed and grew highly. Ziglar established Ziglar's Training Systems based in Carrollton, Texas U.S.A where he is the Chairman and employs other persons working for him. The company is noted in offering sales, motivation and customer service training programmes to multiple companies and agencies. A wonderful feat he achieved through the instrumentality of the God factor.

The success story of Fanny Crosby manifested in the awesome power of God. A blind Christian mother; who lived for 95 years (1820-1915). A well known Christian song writer; of our time. She was nurtured with Christian virtues and had deep relationship with God and developed high level of inspiration to write many songs. Also married a blind husband for 44 years. They had a child who died in infancy. Her musical impact recorded that she wrote and produced about 200 songs each year. It is also on record that she wrote more than 8000 religious poems. Songs like Pass me not oh Lord, Blessed Assurance, Rescue The Perishing, To God Be The Glory… etc were her songs production.

John Wesley, a Christian and preacher of Christ gospel who founded Methodist Church also built a success story of his life. His Methodism led the way for many

Social and Industrial reforms (political and economic assignments) in England which eased the burdens of the people. He was also in the vanguard of supporting William Wilberforce in his fight against Slave Abolition. He came this far because of the influence of God in his life; thus he built success in life.

Also Pastor Vincent N. Paul built success of his life. An author of Persistence Works, a Captain (Military Chaplain) in the United States Army and President of Vincent Paul Ministries International. He gave his life to Christ at the age of 13 years in August 1985, and later answered the call into God's ministry.

Today he has published six books in his books on Persistence Book Series and has finished working on 10 others in the Persistence Series Books. He is at present a multi-gifted, motivational and notable preacher, teacher, healing evangelist, military Chaplain, prolific author and publisher.

Dr. Vincent also publishes persistence work in E- newsletter sent out weekly to several thousands of people in over 150 nations. He is the author of the book- **"Don't Be Discouraged"** (in this book he cited over 40 people who persisted and succeeded in life Vincent acknowledged that God inspires him to write and he writes by the grace of God. He stated thus **"When I was undergoing my undergraduate studies, I never knew I would become a writer. I grew up to discover that I was into writing. I grew up to discover that I was into writing ministry. The more I write, the more the gifts flourish".**

The above proves that God is the source of building one's success in life. Your achieving success or walking into greatness takes place here on planet earth. The earth is a creation of God. Your personality is a creation of God. Thus the first principle toward developing one's success is walking in line with God's power.

CHAPTER FOUR

THE MIND OF ACHIEVERS.

Any person who takes the journey of success becomes an achiever. Achievers are noted as those people who have the mind or capacity to succeed. Everybody desires to achieve success and greatness, but not all have the willingness or capacity to pursue same. The capacity therefore to do so is the heart. The mind brings out the inner strength in man to build success empires. The heart brings out the creative ingenuity in one to succeed. The heart also manifests those characters that draw or pull together those values that aid one to build success. The success recoded gives great sense of belonging to the achiever.

The mind of an achiever could be attained in any profession; sports, religious works, academics, politics, literary world, technology, public speaking, business, event management etc. Whatever success recorded is a manifestation of a function of the performance of activity of a willing mind which must be seen as to champion the growth of human race and societal development.

The heart in human beings stands out great. The heart directs the cause of action in one. In human body, the heart pumps blood to other parts of the body, and if it ceases the body become dead. In the Holy Bible, it is recorded that even though opposition comes on our ways, we should not allow our heart to fret away. (Psalm 27:3). This underscores the importance attached to a mind that wants to succeed; such mind should not be dispelled nor fear in spite of trials and challenges.

Therefore, the mind desirous of achieving greatness must be prepared spiritually and physically; spiritually because one is already charged to succeed. The spiritual is the God factor in recording greatness.

For the physical, one must show great interest to work towards building success in life. The physical is the take off stage. It is the time to take the step of faith towards a course of building success story in life.

Confidence is paramount to any mind that wants to achieve. The person whose mind achieves is the one who will be ready to sacrifice, who will be ready to work, who must plan. In addition, anybody who wants to build success in life must be determined in a chosen profession, the person should also persevere.

History has records of persons who positioned their minds to excel in spite of difficulties and challenges and they include Henry Ford (founder of Ford Motors), Dr. Ben Carson (world renowned neurosurgeon), Alexander Hamilton (a founding father of the USA and 1st Secretary of the Treasurer), Brian Tracy (Author, Conference Speaker), Dr. Chris E. Kwakpovwe (a Nigerian Bishop, Pharmacist, Author), Joyce Meyer (Author, Bible Teacher, Preacher, Conference Speaker), Michael Phelps (Winner of a Total of 23 Olympics Gold Medals in Swimming in 2004, 2008, 2012 and 2016) etc.

Some of the factors that determine or shape the mind of success builders include:

VISION PLAN: The mind of every achiever start with a clear objective(s) of what to achieve in life; even when a mistake has been made due to lack of mentorship or guidance, the correction adopted follows defined plans to achieve the goals. The stated goal is powered by great passion. Dr. Mike Adenuga, GCON; a Nigerian entrepreneur and Chairman of Globacom, would not have carved a niche in the telecommunication world if not that he tenaciously developed mind of an achiever. His initial attempt to acquire and operate the Global System of Mobile did not go through as the conditional license and frequencies granted to him in 1999 were revoked, and he lost the deposit of $20 million mandatory deposit.

However, Dr. Adenuga kept his vision plan alive in spite of setbacks. In August 2002, he bided for the second National Operator and deposited another $20 million through Nigerian Communication Commission and this time he won. As at 2016, Globacom is a major indigenous and private telecommunication company and in addition the first to introduce per second billing in the telecommunication business in Nigeria, a clear demonstration of the power of vision employed by a mind poised to build success in life.

BELIEF IN YOUR SELF: Success builders have great faith in God and in themselves. They believe that God has endowed them with traits with which to succeed. They are aware that God has not given them the spirit of fear, but the spirit to succeed in life. Their steps radiate confidence with which to win. In any endavour they also exhibits inner strength and by so doing attract wonderful public image on their side towards their goals of life..

DETERMINATION: Success builders are highly determined persons. Success builders are aware that obstacles and difficulties exist. They know they can fail, and can only move ahead to succeed if they are determined in the spirit which radiates in the outside of one. If not for determination, history would not have recorded a positive place for Abraham Lincoln, who failed election in USA up to seven times before emerging as the President of USA. For Abraham Lincoln's determination, he is studied in world history.

EDUCATION AND APPLICATION OF KNOWLEDGE: Achievers avail themselves the opportunity to acquire education and apply same accordingly. They expose themselves to reading periodicals and books; which inculcate in them values of achieving success in life. These periodicals and books go a long way to shape their thought and speed up their energies towards advancing the course of humanity and society through accomplishments. Pastor John C. Maxwell; a known Pastor, Author and Conference Speaker, admitted that his father who exposed him to reading books and attending professional courses prepared him early in life.

Building success in life attested to by the society is reserved for the people with the mind of an achiever. The heart of an achiever is positioned to confront challenges as to reach desired goals. Every mind desirous of achievements has a prize; this has remained the driving force of all great people who built success story line.

CHAPTER FIVE

BUILDING SUCCESS IN A PERSONALITY

Vision, energy, determination, focus, patience, discipline, perseverance are key values employed by any person who is eager to become a success story in life. The world has remained a challenging place, and only those who dare will conquer. Negative or hostile environment will continue to exit; hence we should not allow that to deter us in our pursuit to success and greatness in our chosen profession.

It is evident that no nation or human race has ever witnessed continuously friendly environment without setbacks, but those (including nations and persons) that succeeded are those who made self-discoveries and marrying same with determination in spite of the prevalent circumstances of their time to attain greatness.

Growths of Countries were achieved by men who believed in their cause, and pursued same with doggedness and built success in life. Late Dr. Nelson Rolihlahia Mandela (alias Madiba) was highly celebrated because of his persistent and energetic roles in ending apartheid regime in South Africa. Late Lee Kuan Yew (former Singaporean leader and elder statesman) was adored because of how he brought Singapore to political and economic lime light.

For history to record men who achieved success in life, they remained focused, frontal and determined in their chosen endavour. Thus, the power to conquer is within the thought process vide a defined road map.

For any personality to achieve success in any chosen field of endeavour including technological advancement, politics, academics, sports, business, writing, skilled and unskilled professions, religious activities etc attested to by the people, thus impacting positively in the society, the personality must remain courageous.

Winning personality life is built around obstacles, unfriendly environment, trials, failures and errors. But in individual boldness, self-will, dogged determination, perseverance and organized planning lies success.

The person, who succeeds in life, can do it with or without formal education but it requires individual drives and positive mind set internalized by the individual in his chosen profession, thus creating value in the society.

The winning person develops great trust in the Supreme God and develops great interests in fervent prayers to discover and develop talents and skills endowed with.

The conquering personality must develop the virtues of accomplishments amongst which are the God factor, vision, courage, hard work and perseverance.

The person with the drive to succeed avoids dream killers in his life pursuits. The winning personality is aware that God created us to become a success. When we achieve success the societies we live in will also become a success story. From creation, God charged us to go into the world and take dominium. Taken dominium is asserting our authority on this planet earth. The few who have discovered this early in life are today reckoned with as personalities that have achieved greatness. These achievers have through ideas generation changed the face of this planet earth.

Therefore, to live a life of personality accomplishments and greatness, we must avoid dream or vision killers.

In addition, in other to become a successful personality, one must take action on something. When an idea has been generated, such an idea is achievable. Napoleon Hill said **"an idea that is conceived is achievable"**. What has killed our ideas to become a success is our lack of will power and discipline to pursue such an idea. All what we see today as achievements recorded by men and appreciated by all came into being as products of action taken by people. Our brain cells is said to be about 5 billion brain cells, are endowed in us by God to achieve excellence in a chosen or particular area , which we must develop and pursue through taken action.

People who have achieved success and developed their personalities are aware that to realize our dreams or ideas of our hopeful projects, career, vocation etc, we must endavour to have self conviction towards our ideas, we must be resourceful, we must be ready to manifest out one self and deal with our handicaps as well.

Finally, successful personalities have implicit faith in God; He that makes all things possible and who have also given us power to become a success in life will see us through. God created us to become a success. When we achieve success, the societies we live in will also become a success story. From creation, God charged us to go into the world and take dominium. Taken dominium is asserting our authority on this planet earth. The few personalities who have discovered this early in life are today reckoned as great successful people.

CHAPTER SIX.

BUILDING SUCCESS THROUGH THE POWER OF ACTION

Pablo Piscasso said **"Action is the foundation key to all success".** Taken definite action or work in a particular course is the key to build success in life. Many achievers have also noted that without definite action no one achieves positive thing. Becoming successful in life is not a wish, but a thing to be worked for with one's creativity, determination, energy etc. Achieving success require planning and the corresponding strategy to work as to actualize one's dream. Action or work reveals one's potentials in life.

The Holy Bible recognized the importance of work (action) in many Biblical references. Genesis 2:2-3 says **"By the seventh day God had finished the work he had been doing; so on the seventh day he rested from all his work. And God blessed the seventh day and made it holy, because on it he rested from all the work of creating that he had done"**. In addition, Genesis 2: 15 states **"The Lord God took the man and put him in the Garden of Edem to work it and take care of it".** Some other Biblical references on work (action) include; Philippians 2:13, John 4: 34, John 5:7, Mathew 25:16 etc.

If you read further Genesis between Chapters 14 and 20, you will discover that Abraham took action (work). He dug wells, built a massive livestock portfolio, amassed commodities in gold and silver and eventually turned the barren land scape into a blossoming desert.

Taken action or working in a project is a key to building success or achieving greatness and these occupies great space in the minds of authors, entrepreneurs, administrators, professionals etc.

Dr. Napoleon Hill and C. Harold Keown (both author of Succeed And Grow Rich Through Persuasion) opined that **"Imagination alone is not enough to insure success. Millions of people have imagination and built plans that would easily bring them both fame and fortune, but those plans never reach the decision stage. It takes a definite decision. The man of decisions gets what he goes after, no matter how long it takes, no matter how difficult the task. The man of decision cannot be stopped. The man of indecision cannot be stopped. Take your own choice".**

Brian Tracy (author and conference speaker) in his book-"The Power of Self Confidence", writing on action stated thus: **"The real difference between the winners and losers in life is the difference between taking action and making excuses. It is between the people who do and the people who talk about doing. It is between the movers and shakers and those who just watch the world go by. Perhaps, our greatest responsibility to yourself is to become a person of action- to act yourself into feeling the emotions that are consistent with high performance".**

The author of this book- James N. Okere has also thought deep about this and noted that taken action towards a task is of paramount importance; thus I developed the "**BASATA SUCCESS PRINCIPLE**"; Begin Action/ Activity. Start Action/ Activity. Take Action/ Activity. This is one sure way of moving towards life accomplishments.

Michael Phelps winner of a total 23 Olympic gold medals in swimming in 2004, 2008, 2012 and 2016 said **"I wouldn't say anything. I think that everything is possible as long as you put your mind to it and put the work and time into it".**

In the article, "How to be an Everyday Olympian", Michael Viradi; Trainer, Keynote Speaker and Author stated thus **"It takes more than desire or dream to be the best. It also takes hard work".**

In an article, "If You Don't Ask, You Don't Get", Dr. Merritt Jones, author, Mentor, Consultant and Keynote Speaker stated **"It makes it clear that we have a role to play in creating the life we desire which includes an action some of us tend to avoid".**

Also, Anthony Robbins, author of "Unlimited Power", stated **"In essence, if we want to direct our lives, we must take control of our consistent actions. It is not what we do once in a while that shapes our lives, but what we do consistently".**

Dr. Myles Munroe, Author, Pastor and Conference Speaker in his book, "The Principle and Power of Vision" identified the issue of work as a source of building success when he stated that **"The second thing through which God provides for our visions is our work. When you decide to move forward with your dream, it will often take a great amount of work".**

Preston Vanderven, an online marketer, writing on "5 Life Changing Lessons from Tony Robbins (an American entrepreneur, author and philanthropist)", stated that one of the lessons he identified in Robbins success story is; **"Action is the key to success".** Also, Preston Vanderven further identified the importance of action towards success, and in his article "How To Take Consistent Action" stated that **"Maybe the biggest problem people have is that they don't take consistent action over a long time period".**

Action or work involves taken risk, thus Leo Bascagilla stated **"A risk must be taken because the greatest hazard in life is to risk nothing".**

On the other hand, Ajah Mishara, motivational speaker and coach opines that **"No matter where you are, one thing is sure if you have absolute motivation to go ahead in life, you can achieve absolute success".**

Eva Arissani, author of New Moi New life, Inspirational/ Motivational/Business Speaker and Transformational Coach; in his write up on abundance; stated thus: **"To attract abundance, take positive, constructive actions...Take a constructive action towards realizing that abundant life".**

The author of this book- James Ngozi Okere in his book "You Too Can Be Great", identified action as key to achieving greatness. The author wrote further; **"Nobody will do it for you. But when you begin, help must come from God, and some human beings. He added, the will power to succeed lies in one powering himself into action".**

One who wants to be successful must take practical action. It was out of desire and power of action that Steve Wonder a blind man became a great musician in United States of America.

Those who want to be successful must discipline themselves so as to become champions in their field of endeavour. Successful people labour, and wait for result that will eventually come. These classes of people take the initiative for a task, and keep their eyes on the achievements to reckon with.

Men who want to be successful don't see giant, rather they see a land flowing with milk and honey. They imbibe values that would make one become successful like; goal setting, creating energy, maintaining positive mental attitude to life, embrace hard work etc.

Finally, successful people discover their talents and work hard to develop them accordingly.

CHAPTER SEVEN.

FOLLOW YOUR DREAM

In the journey towards building success in life; Ideas and dreams rule the world. To drive your dream, you must understand how others succeeded in life. All living beings created have idea or ideas of what he would want to achieve. These ideas are what rule the world according to Napoleon Hill. One's idea is a dream that has not yet manifested physically.

Ideas are spiritual in nature; our activating such idea makes it a physical value; this is the challenge of any person who would want to build success on this planet earth. The pen we use to write is a product of idea. The papers we use to write are product of ideas generated by persons. Your dream which is your vision is powered via preparations and taken actions towards proper execution. The television some people watch upwards of one, two, four, six, eight, ten or more hours is a product of human idea; developed by persons we regard together as being successful.

Therefore, everybody is endowed with ideas. Everybody is a carrier of a dream for a particular purpose towards advancing humanity. Those who power their dream are courageous, bold and adventurous towards life accomplishments. Persons who reign today are people who dared and developed their dreams with concrete progrmme of action. They are men, women and youths who faced oppositions but with courage surmounted same accordingly. They marched forward believing in God. To succeed in promoting their dreams, they held their faith and confidence in God. These men, women and youths knew that fear existed, but they built their confidence in God, and did many things afraid; thus they succeeded.

In powering one's dream towards building success story, one critical factor is to define what one wants to achieve on this planet earth. Your idea should be in line with God's purpose and agenda, aligning same with one's gifts and talents.

I have identified three groups of people; the first are those who are naturally inspired and daring in life. This group starts pushing their dreams out early in life. The second group are mentored or encouraged to take off with their life endavours. The third and probably the last are those who would discover themselves much later in life. In all, what is important in powering one's idea is for one to discover God's purpose in life; this is a sure way to succeed in life.

To power your dream, you must identify where you are now and make adjustments, think deep of what you are, what you have been doing, what you take keen interest in, available gifts and talents with you. Therefore, start with a new mind set towards what you want to achieve in life. In such life pursuits, endavour to remain focus, courageous, patient, etc.
To further pursue your life dream, you should have in your inner being what Napoleon Hill called Tenacity of Purpose; that is having the knowledge of what you want and the determination to pursue same.

If not for dream pursuit, history would not have recorded Thomas Carlyle as the author of the French Revolution book. Carlyle after working for two years, produced the manuscript of his book, sent same to his friend John Staut Mill for proof-reading. In the process, Mill lost the manuscript, but Carlyle after feeling bad about this development, later consoled himself, and powered himself into his dream project to become the author of the French Revolution book and in this regard built success identity.

The mind that has dream for accomplishment of a task would eventually succeed. Powering your mind on your stated task will provide the magic wand for accomplishment. This calls for consistent focus which leads to pressing on which has solved the problems of the human race.
Thomas Edison failed several times in his quest to provide man with electric bulb. But in spite of Edison's predicaments he remained focused with his dream and eventually succeeded, thereby adding value to human development.

Through your dream, you are to show yourself to the world through your accomplishments. Nothing succeeds than one working to see his dream come through. You must decide to power your dream through locating your God-given talents in order to add value to the society. Pursuits of one’s dream leads to achieving victory in inches in the short run, and in miles in the long run. If you have the dream to manifest humility of life with which to influence the society as Mahatma Gandhi did to influence Indians, continue with such dream.
You might have a dream to defend the downtrodden as Chief Gani Fawehinmi (a Nigerian lawyer) is noted for.

You might have the dream to write as to influence individuals and societies; to achieve such dream you must push the idea forward as Benjamin Franklyn (American Man of Letters) was noted for. In spite of opposition he faced even from his brother, towards developing his writing talents, he continued and ended up achieving his dream of being a successful and renowned author in the world.

Florence Nightingale, born into a wealthy family in London, delved into her dream project; the nursing profession contrary to the expectations of her wealthy parents who never supported her nursing profession. Through her dream in nursing programme and interactions she had with the sick, she developed and published notes on how hospitals should be operated. Florence's determination influenced the nature and structure of today's hospital management; a clear manifestation of one following her dream in a bid to build success in life.

CHAPTER EIGHT

DEVELOP YOUR PERSONALITY

Institutions are developed by personality. Personality is the character inherent in a person. Personality includes values internalized by one which works towards developing a person and society at the same time. A developed personality is a recognized person; a person imbued with trust, honesty, vision and sincerity of purpose. The personality of a person also includes those traits persevered in a course of action to excel in life.

A developed personality is the driving force towards excellence in life pursuits. Accomplished personality is not dwarfed by difficult situations; they continue to move forward positively as to influence society. Thus, in the process of building success in life, one's personality could be developed in many ways amongst which are:

LIFE OF VISION: **"Something can manifest, it must first be visualized"** says Adolfo Torres. In developing life of vision, we visualize what we want or a career or profession one wants to pursue in life. Some people are luckier to be granted a life of vision by God, while some are mentored to pursue same early in life. Many others live a life not defined or lacking in purpose until woken up. Life of vision backed up with action excels a person to stardom in life. In spite of difficulties and challenges one passes through, a person who have discovered and remained focus with his dream, builds success in life and the society reckons with.

BE INITIATIVE: Anybody who wants to achieve or live a life of success and emulation must have the capacity to initiate activities towards his identified life goals. The mind power must be developed to become creative. Creativity gives insights which turn dormant ideas into activity driven. This is in line with what James Allen said **"Through his thoughts, man holds the key to every situation and contains within himself that transforming and regenerative agency by which he may make himself what he wills".** Through being initiative new brands are created that adds value to society thus improving the person(s) behind such action.

DEVELOP YOUR TALENTS: Talent discovery and development is a sure way to build success in life and hence improve the personality of a person. Knowing the importance of this Dr. Myles Munroe a well known pastor, author and public speaker said **"Anyone who develops his gifts will become a community".** Also Dr. Ben Carson, a neurosurgeon and world known role model for the youths on talent said **"If you recognize your talents, use them appropriately, and choose a field that uses those talents, you will rise to the top of your field".**

If somebody discovers his talents and aligns same towards his education or profession, the person excels greatly. However, if one discovers his talents after acquiring his education, the person would also excel, if he eventually develops his talents.

Dr. Walter Lomax a successful physician in Philadelphia U.S.A also recorded many great achievements in life; including having up to seven successful clinics run professionally. However, Dr. Water Lomax had a great talents and insights on how businesses work. In demonstrating his talents he became a consultant for many businesses and government agencies that profited and had tremendous growth from his consultancy, by this achievements he has expanded his personality in the society.

INCULCATE SELF CONFIDENCE: Without self confidence nobody can develop tremendously in life. With self confidence one manifest himself and put into action activities that transforms a person towards adding value to the society. A person with self confidence confronts fears and discouragements with tenacity of purpose towards his dream or goals in life.

George Bernard Shaw built himself and rose to the top through manifesting self confidence in his writing potentials. His mother was a music teacher earning a pittance, and he as a boy worked in an office to supplement the family income. He later resigned his office work, and having discovered himself developed great confidence and took to writing.

Initially, for many years it was not easy for his works to be accepted and published by the newspapers and magazines. But he remained resolute and kept his fighting spirit alive despite successive failures. George B. Shaw remained confident that one day he would succeed, thus he continued to strive towards unlocking his writing talent as to build success story of his life. After some years, a few of his novels were published, but sales were very poor. He did not loose hope and continued writing until he broke the jinx through writing, and became an internationally acclaimed playwright, who won Nobel Prize for literature by building himself and unlocking his potentials.

REMAIN PERSISTENT: Successful men do not quit. Persons who are quitters do not achieve anything. They are not reckoned in life history. Personalities that have realized their dreams of life remained persistent in their pursuit. They visualized the end product of the task before them, and remained resolute with their vision.

Pastor Vincent N. Paul; an author of Persistence Works, a Captain (Military Chaplain) in the United States Army and President of Vincent Paul Ministries International discovered the negative powers of persistence when he said **"the primary message of persistence work is for everyone to refuse to give up in the face of challenges or storms of life".** To remain persistent we must not allow discouragement to become a tool to abort one's goals.

A LIFE OF COMMITMENT: Dr. Walter Doyle Staples, author of "Think Like a Winner" stated **"There can be no great success without great commitment".** In any positive life endavour, one must be highly committed, developing the I Can Spirit towards a course of action. Commitment goes with passion and positive mental attitude to excel. Commitment is decisive action taken to achieve.

Stephen Skinner a successful pharmacist had a dream to help other Christian entrepreneurs succeed greatly in life, and to do it, he developed a programme tagged "Life Message". Following his commitment spirit towards the programme, he launched a speaking, coaching and writing business. He committed himself and got his Life Message turned into a book titled "The 100 x Life: 7 Simple Daily Habits That will Transform Your Life, Unlock Your Greatest Potential, and Create a Life Beyond Your Wildest Dream".

Finally, building success in life is great virtue that transforms one to prominence leading to individual and societal growth.

CHAPTER NINE.

BECOME AN INFLUENCER.

Those who influence the world today, are those who have built success story around their lives. These influencers now serve as role models in our societies. They are men and women who have accomplished great tasks attested to by the people and society. They are persons who have through their successes influenced society. These people are highly appreciated and made reference to.

Men who can inspire or influence their environment are men that have discovered themselves and dominated their community. They are persons who are written about. They are men painters would want to draw inscription of what they represent. Men who dominate their environment exist in various aspect of the society including in governance, economic, scientific discovery, sports, management, leadership, religious institutions etc. The processes making it possible for one to become influencer in the society includes as follows; Passion to serve, leadership, talent discovery and development, writing etc.

PASSION TO SERVE: Many are abound who have used their passion to serve, and using same to influence the people. Mahatma Gandhi was well known as somebody who had great passion to serve, coupled with his simple life style with which he used to influence the entire environment of India. The death of Gandhi did not stop the Indians from acknowledging who he was till date.

Mother Theresa also used his passion to serve the people to influence her environment. She worked hard to get many charity/ social rehabilitation institutions established under his support. Mother Theresa was a truly living human being with an infinite capacity to care for and support the sick and dying people of Calcutta and others.

LEADERSHIP: Through leadership, societies have been influenced positively by people who built success life. History has records of those who have used leadership positions to inspire life and confidence into the people.

Today in United States of America, people still records the roles of Thomas Jefferson; the former third United States of American president and a foundational member of the mastermind team that championed American independence. The primary role he played as the writer of the declaration of independence of America is spoken till date.

In addition, the leadership provided by Church Hill the war time Prime Minister of Britain is still influencing Britain as much reference about him are still made till date.

Nelson Mandela, former President of South Africa was one man whose succeess story around leadership acumen became extra-ordinary in the world. Even when he was no more, he is still being highly celebrated; that 18th July is celebrated as Nelson Mandela day all over the world as declared by United Nations. By all these feet these men mentioned built success life.

Through talents people become a success in life. Dr. Ben Carson stated that **"If you recognize your talents, use them appropriately and choose a field that uses those talents, you will rise to the top of your field".** Hence, you can also influence your environment through discovery and developing of your talents. Many have used their sports, administrative, writing, selling talents etc to change the course of history.

We speak much about Michael Jordan of America who performed well in the basket ball spots. His roles have influenced many basket ball enthusiasts and others who have also learnt team work spirit from him. In Nigeria, many people have also been influenced by the activities of footballers like Kanu Nwankwo, Jay Jay Okocha etc.

Talent discovery and development is so important that Dr. Myles Munroe a well known pastor, author and public speaker said **"Anyone who develops his gifts will become a community".**

Writing distinguishes one. It takes one to higher level. Every writer who continues and never quit reaches a remarkable heights in life. Today, mention Dr. C Maxwell, Prof. Wole Soyinka, Dr. Myles Muroe, Brian Tracy one will definitely mention books authored by them.

Mention Fanny Cross and Bernard Shaw; one's mind runs to the works written by them. These writers or authors are not forgotten as their works and accomplishments are always being remembered and cited accordingly. These writers have influenced the society in that even after their death; their works are still being spoken about.

Mention Charles Dickens, you remember one of his works titled “Oliver Twist”. Mention Dimgba Igwe; a Nigerian, you remember his journalistic works as well.

Finally, all these influencers who act as role models have used their words of wisdom and quotes to build humanity. Their wisdom expressed vide quotes have added values to people even centuries of years they have left this planet earth.

CHAPTER TEN.

WORK TO BECOME AN IMPACT PERSON

An impact person works towards building a success story line. The person influences people towards success without coercion or force. By their method they drive people to achieve a common purpose. Impact person creates a platform for team work or spirit towards accomplishing task(s).

Impact person is a loving, caring, admired and respected person. He is a sincere person. An impact person is positively discussed and studied as to use his core values of life to advance society. He fears God, is valuable, committed to a cause, highly sacrificial and demonstrates initiatives.

God who created man in his own image from creation demonstrated His impact nature in the lives of the people when He amongst others created the sun, moon, rainfall, air, river, sand, trees etc. Thus, anybody becoming an impact person should radiate the glory of God on this planet earth. In the words of Dr. Myles Munroe, he opined that **"When we exercise our creativity we are displaying the God like attributes and nature He placed in us"**.

As creators of God, who are desirous of building success story, we are to manifest positive life style leading to positive thinking, thereby living a peaceful life. In addition, an impact person should conquer his world through his activities. The person must put his ideas, skills, talents and abilities into action towards building a successful life. Also an impact leader should be diligent in his works/ services as to dominate his environment.

William Wilberforce as a Christian entered into the British Parliament at 21 years after a Cambridge education. Wilberforce developed love and concern for others and subsequently set his affection upon a cause that would affect the destinies of millions of people all over the world. He initiated and championed the formation of a law to abolish slave trade. For 46 years he fought this battle and won. The whole world was made a better place and the entire society and man was given a better code conduct as a result of his campaign and victory. What an impact life William Wilberforce lived towards building a successful life style.

Dr. Oswald Smith built his success life throughout the entire globe with evangelism; winning souls for Christ. His popular motto includes **"The supreme task of the church is the evangelization of the world"**. He travelled wide to preach including Jamaica, New Zealand, Russia, Great Britain and many European countries. He won many souls and once it was said he fainted while preaching the gospel. Even when suffering from attacks of malaria he preached the gospel as well. Dr. Oswald preached in more than sixty-six countries. Even with that outing he was quoted to have said "I am not satisfied". Today his accomplishments have challenged many in this respect; what an impact success living.

In addition, Martin Jr. Luther King lived on this planet for 39 years and within this period he lived a success life. The time he was born was when there were segregation and chains of discrimination in the United States of America. He was disturbed by the discrimination suffered by blacks, he then took the cause to champion the end through his group he formed Southern Christian Leadership Conference (SCLC) and civil rights movement to end racial segregation in America. Through his efforts, he saw to the signing of civil rights bill in 1964 and voting rights Act in 1965 which gave leverage to blacks and subsequently banned discrimination in public accommodation, employment and labour unions. With a life of success he developed; he built great many around his vision to fight against discrimination and ills in the society. Martin Luther king is still being made a reference point till date; a mark of success life.

Chinedu Nsofor, a Nigerian graduated from the University of Nigeria, Enugu State Eastern Nigeria. He is 28 years as at year 2018. Chinedu Nsofor set his vision to live a successful life and thus identified his goals to pursue as to impact life in his environment. While at the University he developed his dream project- WORK WHILE IN SCHOOL; a programme designed to encourage our undergraduate to start early to think on their future plan of life. As at present, he has secured partnership with some organizations. His idea has started creating impact in the Nigerian Society.

Living a life of impact is a worthy cause to be pursued by all as to advance one's personality and humanity.

CHAPTER ELEVEN.

PRESS ON TO YOUR MARK

To build success in life one should remain unstoppable. Forward ever, backward never is the mind set of successful people and if we internalize same and put it into action, we would advance in life. It means nothing would keep us from not realizing our God given potentials on this planet earth. No wander Martin Luther King Jnr., a black American who worked hard in advancing the cause of humanity in the world via eradicating segregation said **"If we can't fly, we must run, if we can't run, we must walk, and if we can't walk we must crawl and if can't crawl, by all means we must keep moving"**. What a wonderful thought from such a personality, who sacrifices his life while working for humanity and died at the age of 39 years.

Building success in life is a difficult thing, thus we should strive to at least crawl to move forward in our identified vision. The time we are in now is the time to think deep and persevere to move on with our God given potentials on this planet earth. The time we are in now is a time to make new discoveries of our lives; that is the primary and most fundamental issue if we must build success story of our life. Discovering and developing our selves is the primary issue of the time. It goes with discovering our potentials, gifts, talents etc endowed us by God. Success builders look beyond their challenges and trials and look for opportunities in there. No wander; Sunny Ojeagbese, a Nigerian inspirational writer and publisher said **"Adversity goes hand in hand with opportunities, which is one secret of success people don't know".**

In the Holy Bible, we have records of many who saw adversities but remained calm and kept pressing on to success. Moses, Jesus Christ, Daniel, Paul etc demonstrated calm and moved forward in crises. To keep moving, we must go closer to God and pray continually to enable us receive insights and creative ways to develop our potentials. God in Psalm 34; 19 assured that **"Many are the affiliations of the righteous, but the Lord will deliver you out of then all".**

To remain unstoppable and move forward, is to not give up to the challenges of the present time. The book "Tough Times Never Last, But Tough People Do" is a book written by Dr. Robert Shuller; an American Pastor, Author and Speaker. The book was written when there was serious economic depression in America. The book gave hope and vision to Americans, that those who remained persistent in their chosen field were positively impacted in their life pursuits because they kept moving forward with their ideas. Dr. Robert's articulation, became a success story line for generations yet unborn.

No matter the challenges we face including economic one, our not given up would lead us to achieving greater accomplishments. However, on our journey to build success, what we need is to pray, persevere, never give up and keep moving forward with whatever our hands find doing.

In our journey to build success we should believe that one day the difficult period will be over and success recorded accordingly. To remain unstoppable and press on, means we should display positive mind set and continue to strive with whatever positive thing our hands find doing to improve our life and personality as to impact society.

The person desirous to accomplish, should inculcate the values of re-inventing geared towards bringing out the best in us which comes from God who blessed us with various gifts and potentials waiting for our working on their manifestation; which when accomplished, glorifies our God.

In our journey to achieve success, is also a period to think deep about one's potentials and talents deposited in us. This is the time to put into use our gifts and potentials as to manifest the greatness in us. As we press on, we should have our ultimate faith in God, pray to Him to change things for the better. Looking up to God will energize our spirit being to manifest fruits that would keep us right with God and in so doing we receive insights and ideas on what to do as to change our story for the better.

My humble self, James Okere has kept pressing on, improved my reading capacity to drive myself towards my life goals via new line of positive thought including developing the passion leading to my being in a position to discuss on issues of inspiration, mentorship, leadership and self developing values. The inspirational website, www.inspireforgreatness.com which I develop and blog in is as a result of my resolution not to give up. Today, following the discovery of importance of reading, I now advocate strongly on the need for people to read including promoting **Donate a Book Project.** I have also authored three e-Books; "You Too Can Be Great (Core Value Self- Re- Orientation)", 2017, "Developing Yourself", 2017, "How To Excel In Life", 2017, all by Lulu Publishers, USA.

As to further remain unstoppable, since year 2015, I have maintained regular newspaper columns (in Imo State, Eastern Nigeria); titled: **Inspirational Values.** I have also established a social service organization called Inspire Foundation (IF). I have also powered the establishment of Inspire Foundation (IF) Leadership and Mentorship Academy (an online programme). The above would not have been possible if I did not believe in myself and at the same time change my thinking; taken a firm decision to press on.

There was this story of a roommate of Dr. Myles Munroe when they were in college. The name of this his roommate is Steve. When Steve was completing his college programme, he ran out of money, he thinkered on what to do as to build success story line. Steve then borrowed a friend's lawn mower and began to mow people's lawns to earn some money to continue his education. The story continued that after Steve graduation he was making more than $100,000 a year from his lawn mowing company he established out of adversity. To build our success story, we should keep moving forward no matter the situation; this requires strong will power, faith in God, perseverance etc.

We should reflect on issues challenging us and endavour to pray as to generate ideas and energy towards tackling them. Your idea to introduce a particular social reform could be started. Your idea to start writing a book or writing an article or news talk or blogging on a particular issue should be pursued, as you never can tell where your next success and breakthrough comes from. Your idea to join with one or two or more friends to start a new line of business should not be delayed further, but to start no matter how small. Recall that the Holy Bible reminded us in the book of Job that we should not discard the days of little beginning.

Having taken up an action, we should persevere and press on. Perseverance brings out the best in us. Before perseverance takes place, one should have been tried. To further press on to the mark, we should remain consistent with that worthy cause of action laid in our hearts as to realize our purpose in life.

CHAPTER TWELVE.

POWER OF COMMITMENT IN BUILDING SUCCESS.

To build success in life you need to develop commitment spirit. Dr. Walter Doyle Staples, author of "Think Like a Winner" stated **"There can be no great success without great commitment".** In any positive life endavour, one must be highly committed, developing the I Can Spirit to the course of action. Commitment goes with passion and positive mental attitude which enable somebody to excel. Commitment is decisive action taken to achieve.

We commit ourselves to identified ideas. By nature we are imbued with ideas or dreams we should pursue when we discover our purpose on this planet earth. Achievements of men are product of commitment. The cars we drive and enjoy, the pen we use to write, the writing papers, the electrical bulbs all came as result of commitment. Commitment works with one remaining focus, persevering and developing courage in the face of challenges.

The ideas or dreams we carry with us towards building success in life can only become a reality if we commit our time, energy and creativity into what we do. A committed person imbued with passion to succeed is always available towards his set goals of life. A committed person does not give up. He believes in pressing on to his goals. Those we celebrate as great persons were men, women and youths who devoted themselves towards their plan of action. These men, women and youths we celebrate now, initially were not given any opportunity to succeed, but they remained resolute because they believed in themselves and in their God given talents and gifts, thus committing their time and energy.

To be committed, we should decide what we really want. We should think deep on our talents and gifts which would support us in realizing God's purpose in our life as to help advance society for the betterment of mankind.

Stephen Skinner a successful pharmacist had a dream to help other Christian entrepreneurs succeed greatly in life, and to do it, he developed a programme tagged "Life Message". Following his commitment spirit towards the success of the programme, he launched a speaking, coaching and writing business. He committed himself and got his Life Message turned into a book titled **"The 100 x Life: 7 Simple Daily Habits That will Transform Your Life, Unlock Your**

Greatest Potential, and Create a Life Beyond Your Wildest Dream". This his successes and achievements were after he committed himself to attend a seminar programme titled- Amplify Workshop organized by Jonathan Miligan which took place in October 2015; and between October 2015 and December 2015 the book came out, and between December 2015 and April 2016 he also wrote and published 3 devotional books as supplements to his core book. His commitment improved highly his personality that created four income streams for him in book sales, speaking opportunities, coaching and online course.

The book sales alone created up to six ways in a month royalty, and in addition added to him speaking opportunities, coaching and online programmes. Within less than 12 months his commitment transformed his personality, thus he built a success story of his life.

Benjamin Franklin showed interest to build a success story in the writing world. Benjamin Franklin longed to write for his older brother's newspaper where he worked as a printing apprentice but his brother refused to let him. Ben wrote stories anyway, under a pen name, "Silence Dogood", a fictional widow who was very opionated, particularly on the issue of the treatment of women. Every letter was stuck under the printing shop's door at night to avoid discovery, and "Silenced Dogood" became wildly popular. After sixteen letters, Ben finally admitted that he was the writer and though he received quite a bit of positive attention from everyone else, his brother only grew angrier. This resulted in Ben receiving beatings and finally running away. Ben never allowed his commitment towards his success drive to die as a result of his brother's attitude.

In line with Benjamin's success building story, he eventually started his own printing shop and took over a newspaper, the Pennsylvania Gazette, which under his supervision became the most successful in the colonies. Benjamin Franklin wrote a lot in influencing Americans that he became known as the "American Man of Letters"; who later knowing the importance of writing in life developed this motivating quote **"Writing is the beginning of all wealth"** Ben's commitment which also brought wonderful public image in his life, led him becoming a successful diplomat in American history, thus he built a success story of his life.

Commitment is a great virtue that transforms one to prominence leading to individual and societal growth. Commitment works greatly with one's potentials in line with one's purpose on this earth.

CHAPTER THIRTEEN.

BECOME THE SUCCESS STORY

The Holy Bible in the book of Matthew 5: 14-16 stated that we are the light of the world. It added let your light shine before men, that they may see your good deeds and praise your father in Heaven. Light is a dominant value on this planet earth. Man therefore can become the light of the world because of his contributions in the society.

Therefore to become the success story is to become a person of value who is emulated as well. It also connotes a person of relevance on this planet earth. To become a success line means that you have developed yourself in a particular area. You are a person sort for in a particular area of life.

On this planet earth, there are diverse and unaccountable areas one can become a success personality for the betterment of the society. These areas include environmental, political, socio-economic, sports, administration, writing, public speaking, computer development and religious works. Other areas one can dominate and become a success include tailoring, cooking, shoe making, crafts, motor repairs etc; the list is endless.

The most important thing is to decide to become a person of relevance and to work towards such vision. To become a success and dominate your environment, you must be in the known. You must study and search for knowledge. Depending the area of your specialization, you can become active in attending conferences and seminars as to further build your capacity and energy towards becoming the success story.

A person who builds success in life has taking pain and made sacrifices to become somebody. The person has taking time to develop his potentials, skills, talents etc. Talent development is one sure way to build success and dominate one's environment. Dr. Myles Munroe; a pastor, author, public speaker etc, said that a person who develops his talents becomes a community. This is true and challenging for everybody.

To become a success story requires energy, courage and strength. It also requires winning spirit. It requires discipline as well.

When we mention people like Brian Tracy, Joyce Mayer, Dr. Ben Carson, Dr. Myles Munroe, Prof. Pat Utomi, Dr. Mike Murdock, Robert Schuller, Dr. Linus Okorie etc, we appreciate them, but if we study them we would be amazed with what they have passed through in life before reaching their present status. In their trying to succeed, they failed, faced rejections and got disappointed on many occasions. Some who are being celebrated today; may have even questioned the reason for their being on planet earth.

Persons who built success life and developed themselves are still being discussed several years they have left this planet earth. Many people are even feeding from the works and accomplishments of these departed persons.

To become the success story in your environment, you must pursue a life of vision. Life of vision is a purposeful life. It is a life of working assiduously in one's chosen career or profession. Some have developed a vision while in secondary and higher institutions, and have equally pursued their dreams gradually; remaining positively.

Dr. Linus Okorie, the President of Guardians of Nations International (GOTIN) developed his passion while he was in secondary school. He continued with such vision while at the University; even when people did not believe in him, but he believed in himself. Today, he is a man that have developed and dominated his environment in the core areas of leadership values and public speaking sphere.

In addition, to dominate one's environment, one must bear the characteristics of an eagle; including courage, boldness and an eye to see genuine opportunity amongst others.

One of the greatest impressionist painters who became a success story himself was named Paul Gauguin. He lived in Paris, had a family and worked in the post office for many years. He developed his core interest in impressionist paintings and in the evenings, he visited the cafes frequently by the impressionist painters of Paris, getting to know them and asking them questions. He was fascinated by painting. The whole idea of painting absorbed all his attention. The vision grew in him and it was all he thought about. And yet with a family and a full time job, there was no way he could devote himself to the painting he wanted so badly to do.

Being powered by his passion to build a success story line, one day in a move that shocked everybody, he gave up his job as a postal inspector, left his family and moved to South Sea Island of Tahiti. There, he began painting as he developed his skill. Through courage and hard work his paintings now are worth hundreds of thousands, even millions, of dollars and they hang in the finest museums in the world. He is considered by many to be one of the most important painters of the last three hundred years.

In a way, he was like Grandma Moses in that he finally decided to follow his heart and concentrate on what he had been interested in for all those years, thus he persevered and encouraged himself that through his works, he ended up building a success of his life. Such similar success awaits a willing and determined person.

CHAPTER FOURTEEN.

MY BLOGGING JOURNEY:

By December 2017, I have spent four years in blogging. In brief blogging is a medium through which one demonstrates his writing skills, talents, abilities etc, thus creating a niche and a platform for the blogger or writer. The development of my website in year 2013 was instrumental to my blogging. I blog in these areas; leadership, mentorship, personality, entrepreneurship and inspirational nuggets. These areas give me joy since my calling is to inspire my readers. The core value of my website is to impact men, women and youths with values of life towards their personal and societal development; this has remained my driving desire.

On the other hand, my blogging vision is to inspire the world with positive values towards raising global leaders for life accomplishments; this I do through my inspiring blog website, www.inspireforgreatness.com

About June 2013 at the University of Nigeria Alumni Association (UNAA) National Executive Committee (NEC) meeting, held at Aba, Abia State Eastern Nigeria was where my blogging idea was conceived. Before then, my two friends-Dr. Joachim Ezeji and Nnamdi Ogwazu had informed me on the need to own a blog since I was a writer; though not yet established. During the UNAA NEC meeting, I shared a room with my friend-Nnamdi Ogwazu, a Journalist, Opinion Analyst, Public Speaker and Founder of an online media outfit; www.imostateonline.com

With him we discussed extensively on my idea; he encouraged me and told me that I have been writing but without core definition (thus, I lacked focus) and that I must define my writing core areas. He further advised I should include entrepreneurship as part of my blog, www.inspireforgreatness.com

What next? When we returned to Owerri Imo State, Eastern Nigeria after the UNAA NEC meeting, I told him to put an advert for a website developer. I told him because he has great interest in internet works and myself was just a beginner.

Nnamdi later placed an advert in the internet using his internet medium. At the end three persons showed interest. We read through their submissions. Ajewole Ayotokunbo application was the last to be read and as his submission was being read, I was attracted to his detail presentations; Nnamdi too expressed the same filling. I followed up this with Nnamdi and after few e-mail exchanges, I contracted Ajewole Ayotokunbo through Nnamdi internet medium.

We briefed Ajewole on what I wanted; he followed me up with more details towards developing my choice blogging website. As at this time, I didn't know much about blogging. Even when I received kudos from people about my blogging works, I still never knew about blogging, but unknowing to me, I was on the right track by the Divine Grace and the Power of God working in me.

Ajewole moved into action, and myself having mentally made up on what I wanted to achieve, also moved into action of reading and writing in my core areas spanning: leadership, mentorship, personality, inspirational nuggets and entrepreneurship.

Between June 2013 and October 2013, I was working hard towards developing my contents and brand, www.inspireforgreatness.com At the time Ajewole was ready for me, I have developed many articles for uploading. All the works got ready for uploading were typed by my lovely wife, Mrs. Adelyn Okere. Later in November 2013, the website blog went public.

Ajewole is a high level professional, reach with the intricacies of computer and internet works for persons and organizations.

As at now, when I look at my website and the contents therein, I keep asking myself; how did I come to this level? I will answer; it is by God's Grace upon me.

Yes, I have developed blogging website, then who and who knows; this brings the issue of marketing the website and my core values to the public throughout the world. I adopted various ways to make the website become visible to the people. At every time, I was thinking on how to move the visibility of the website, each step taken to market the website create another step. From inception till date, though being an intellectual website visits to the website has remained encouraging every day.

My inspirational website team has been supportive to me in various ways. The members include; Emeka Umunnakwe, Smart Ekechukwu, Rev. Emmanuel Okereke, Rev. Sam Duru, Igwe Israel Okezie, Rev. Innocent Osuoha, Tochi Ewunonu, Mrs. Peace Igwe, Zach Uchegbu, Ogaranya, Bright Okere, David Nnamezie Ugowezie and Chima Ezirim. Also worthy of mention is Odinaka

Onwuatuogu; now my online publishing assistant and an upcoming website developer).

The coming of Odinaka into my life in June 2015 was miraculous; a great divine arrangement. Odinaka has been supportive of some development in my website since we met. He played great roles in the publication of my first ever e-Book, "You Too Can Be Great". where he handled the formatting works as to suit the eBook publishers, Lulu Publishers. The same he handled my second (Developing Yourself) and third (How To Excel In Life) e-book publications. Odinaka has great interest in computer and internet services. These books are available via http://www.lulu.com/shop/james-ngozi-okere/you-too-can-be-great/ebook/product-23034358.html, http://www.lulu.com/shop/james-ngozi-okere/developing-yourself/ebook/product-23176780.html, http://www.lulu.com/shop/james-ngozi-okere/how-to-excel-in-life/paperback/product-23359281.html

My blogging journey was instrumental to the publications of these three e-books. Also, through my blogging, the passion to champion the Donate a Book Project as a way to encourage Reading Culture amongst the youth was developed.

Also my wife, Adelyn formed a core team. From inception in year 2013, my wife was instrumental to all the word processor done in the course of promoting my inspirational website; this she did alone till year 2014. Today, the level I have accomplished in computer word processor was courtesy of her assistance and encouragement. Since year 2015, I have handled all my typing works courtesy of my wife's counsel. She once told me, "Dede" (Dede means elder brother; one of the three names she calls me), what you are doing now (blogging) does not require a third party to handle your computer typing works? Her statement has kept me going till date.

My other team members are some of those who have read my blog works and made some remarkable remarks which have remained encouraging to me. These men and women include: Preston Vander ven (an online marketing expert), Monica Chettal (a Transformation Coach and HR Consultant), Wilbur Brown (School Presenter for K-12 Teachers at Mind Streams), Charles Schwab (an entrepreneur), Pastor Austen Nlemchukwu etc.

Also, many authors and writers have been part of my blogging journey for which I am grateful to all of them. These authors and writers include: Napoleon Hill, Brian

Tracy, Pastor John C. Maxwell, Pastor Oral Roberts, Dr. Myles Munroe, Pastor Mike Murdock, Dr. Ben Carson Pastor Benny Hinn and Joyce Meyer. Others are Robert H. Schuller, Norman Vincent Peale, Pastor T.D Jakes, Dr. Chris E. Kwakpovwe, Pastor David Ibiyeomie, Bill Newman, Pastor Joel Osteen, Udo Okonjo, Daniel Ally, Ajah Mishara and many others; some, I have mentioned in my blogging works.

My inspirational website has given me visibility, reputation, platform, a brand name etc. It has also attracted some speaking engagements, consultancy works as well. With my website, I applied for goggle adsense advert which goggle approved after appraisal, a sign of recognition.

With the website, I am now being quoted by readers including students who now make reference to my works. My blogging website also gave me ready platform to advertise my three e-books, "You Too Can Be Great", "Developing Yourself" and "How To Excel In Life".

In addition, through my blogging experience, I spear headed the establishment of Inspire Foundation (IF), Non-Governmental Organization that engages in self Enhancement and Advocacy in these areas: Mentorship, Entrepreneurship, Leadership, Self and Community Development values aimed at developing the youth for self realization and advancement for a better society.

The Inspire Foundation (IF) Leadership and Mentorship Academy (IFLMA), www.inspireforgreatness.com/inspirefoundation whose motto is Purpose Discovery towards Self and Societal Development, is a product of my Blogging Journey.

My Blogging Journey has been by the Grace of God, vision, pain, hard work, patience, determination and hope.

CONCLUSION.

When we have built success story in life, we become champions. Champions all over the world are influencers who equally serve as role mentors. Champions strive to discover their purpose on this planet earth; a message of building success in life. Those that have built success life have gone the extra mile in developing themselves. They are men and women who have accomplished great tasks attested to by the people and society. They are persons who have through their successes influenced society. These people are highly appreciated and made reference to; this is our great challenge.

To Building success in life lead one to learn from challenges and difficult environment. Persons who have recorded success see challenges as tools for greater accomplishments towards human and societal development. These great people who are men, women and youth inspire or influence their environment. They are persons who have discovered themselves and dominated their community. They are persons who are written about. They are men painters would want to draw inscription of what they represent.

These persons who have built success story and dominating their environment exist in various aspect of the society including in governance, economic, scientific discovery, sports, management, leadership etc. This is the challenge we should strive to accomplish in life, a task for one indeed.

BRIEF ON JAMES NGOZI OKERE.

James Ngozi Okere studied Political Science at the University of Nigeria Nsukka, Eastern Nigeria and he is a member of Nigerian Institute of Management (MNIM).

He is also the author of the following books: A Rotary Hand Book For Rotaractors, 1995 Nigeria By The Year 2040 - Path To National Unity And Stability (A Nigerian Thought), 2001, Who Is Who (In Nigeria Fifty Years Of Political Quotes), 2002 and You Too Can Be Great (Core Value Self- Re- Orientation) 2011.

James has many published works on Nigeria's political concepts. He enjoys reading, writing and thinking on developmental issues. His three books are published online- You Too Can Be Great (Core Value Self- Re- Orientation), 2017, Developing Yourself, 2017, How To Excel In Life, 2017, by Lulu Publishers, USA.

Presently, James Okere is the Lead Consultant of Inspire Foundation (IF) Leadership and Mentorship Academy, Author, a Social Entrepreneur and Project Coordinator of Inspire Foundation (IF), an NGO. Inspire Foundation (IF) is involved in educational issues covering self Enhancement and Advocacy in these areas: Mentorship, Entrepreneurship, Leadership, and Self Development values aimed at developing the people-men, women and students/youths for self realization and advancement for a better society.

His professional interest stretches from writing, inspirational blogger, public speaking, and strategic research to leadership development. He is active with community works and development.

In year 2013, Okere developed a website www.inspireforgreatnesss.com the website promotes issues in leadership, mentorship, personality, entrepreneurship, inspirational nuggets, and governance.

Okere is a strong believer in prayers and holds that everybody is somebody. He lives in Owerri, Imo State Eastern Nigeria.

E-mail: jmsokere@gmail.com , +2347035289205, +2348181517688

www.ingramcontent.com/pod-product-compliance
Ingram Content Group UK Ltd.
Pitfield, Milton Keynes, MK11 3LW, UK
UKHW041835200726
13854UKWH00003BA/1142

9 781387 579280